Stations of the Cross

Stations of the Cross

The Story of God's Compassion

Rev. T. Ronald Haney

With illustrations by
Bro. Michael O'Neill McGrath, OSFS

A Herder Parish and Pastoral Book
The Crossroad Publishing Company
New York

The Crossroad Publishing Company
www.CrossroadPublishing.com

Printed in the United States of America

Library of Congress Cataloging-in-Publication Data

Haney, Thomas R.
    The Stations of the Cross : The story of God's compassion /
  by T. Ronald Haney : illustrated by Michael O'Neill McGrath.
      p.   cm.
    ISBN 0-8245-1769-5 (hardcover : alk. paper)
    1. Stations of the Cross.   I. Title.
  BX2040.H267   1999
  232.96 – dc21   98-28761

2   3   4   5   6   7   8   9   10   15   14   13   12   11

Contents

The First Station
Jesus Is Condemned

His silence.
That's what disturbs the most.
It cuts through the savagery of history,
slicing into the very marrow of
brutal, wanton, wasteful killings
like his own.
Condemned, he remains silent.

The Silence of Jesus

Condemned, he remains silent.
He has no need for words.
Words of justification.
Words of retaliation.
Words of logic or passion.

His life spoke for him.
His entire life was the answer to
questions about the expediency of
eliminating those who disturb the good order of political procedure.
"It is better for one man to perish than a whole nation!" (John 11:50).

His whole life was his response to
those who profit from
the hunger,
the starvation,
of millions.
"The food I will give you is my flesh" (John 6:51).

The surrender of his flesh,
the pouring out of his blood:
these proclaimed the answer to
those who crucify with
the sharp words of rash judgments,
the hammer blows of slander,
the splintered wood of gossip,
pricking,
entering, and
lodging in the victim's reputation.
"Judge not lest you be judged" (Matt. 7:1).

Christ, innocent and condemned, is God's word to us.
A word of *freedom.*
A word of *reconciliation.*
A word of *courage.*

Freedom from sin — which holds us back
from becoming all that we can become:
Fully human.
Fully identified with Christ.

Reconciliation — in which forgiveness,
offered and received,
is the experience of God himself,
the bond of our love
expressed in the healing
of fragmented lives.

Courage — strengthening us
to name the inhuman atrocities
committed on behalf of selfish wealth and greedy power.
Empowering us to
change a lifestyle that perpetuates
the poor,
the exploited,
the maimed,
the illiterate,
the starving,
the outcast,
the murdered.

Now the Word stands silent.
A rebuke
to those who enslave by the sheer ugliness of corporate greed;
to those whose vengeance is wrapped in the banner of patriotism;
to those who love to hate, who prey on the misery of the unfortunate,
claiming a sanctimonious logic for their economic manipulation
of people who cannot help themselves.
"Bless and curse not" (Rom. 12:14).

The Word is the only answer.

Few, however, listen.
People are
too busy,
too preoccupied.
They must get ahead even at the expense of another's livelihood.
They must have more,
surrounding themselves with the status symbols of affluence and success.
They must discover new pleasures to fill the same old void in their hearts.
"What does it profit a man if he gain the whole world...?" (Mark 8:36).

9

No need for arguments now.
The victory he seeks is not over his opponents but over death.
Words would be futile.
Only the act of laying down his life can guarantee this victory.

He had made his decision.
He would go up to Jerusalem.
It meant his death.
It meant his final victory.
Let his enemies jeer and blaspheme.
They had heard his words,
and now he will live them to the death.

Now there is nothing but silence.
Does he maintain silence because of the utter uselessness
of trying to enlighten those who prefer the darkness?
Or does he maintain his silence so that the shouts of condemnation
will fade into the dumbstruck realization that so many crimes
are perpetrated with the most self-righteously rationalized motives?
Is his silence the space needed to contemplate the ultimate answer
which is the life of the Word made flesh?

Prayer

Jesus, innocent, condemned, silent, your silence embarrasses me.
I am silent, but not because of the moral eloquence of my life.
The willful timidness of my heart seals my lips.
My silence cries out, "I do not want to get involved."
I am silent because I am afraid that I will have to do what I speak.
I fear that if I do speak out on issues,
take a stand, go against the slogan of the moment,
all that will be left to me will be the journey of the cross.

I don't want that struggle, that mockery, that suffering, that crucifixion.
So I am silent in the hope that I will go unnoticed, be liked by everyone,
be able to live my customary comfortable piety.

Jesus, your silence condemns me because when I do speak up,
it is only to air my hurts over and over to anyone and everyone
who will stop long enough to let me whine and whimper,
even if they are totally uninterested.
I am always the victim. Everyone else is at fault.
The refrain in my dirge of complaints is, "Pity me."

Jesus, true and silent victim,
let the power of your life,
the beauty of your silence,
be my courage.

The Second Station
Jesus Accepts the Cross

The Cross.
Stark.
Frightening—
not so much for what it is
but for what it will become.
An instrument of torture and death.
A Crucifix.
Yet he takes it.

The Willingness of Jesus

Yet he takes it.
He who
"became sin for our sake" (2 Cor. 5:21)
takes the cross
willingly,
graciously,
silently.

This is not resignation.
This is initiative.

The burden of the world's atrocities is laid upon his shoulders.
Sin of all kinds of magnitude and pettiness weigh him down.
"Come to me all you who labor and are burdened
and I will refresh you" (Matt. 11:28).

With this cross he will
liberate us,
free us,
make us whole,
retrieve us from everything that holds us back
from a full and total response to our Father.

There can be no true freedom unless there is death.
"Unless the grain of wheat falls to the earth and dies,
it remains just a grain of wheat" (John 12:24).

We will blossom to full bloom
by our many deaths to self.
Death liberates us for growth.
Sacrifice willingly embraced,
not merely endured,
brings us to the fullness of all God wants us to become.

For him the cross is not the final burden.
It is the ultimate relief.
It is the sign that will contradict
the finest minds as they work together
to bring about the new prosperity,
the economic utopia

wherein there is
no pain,
no suffering,
no inequity,
no Christ.
"Without me
you can do nothing" (John 15:5).

A sign of contradiction
for all those who bleed the masses
to erect and sustain the balance of terror
that guarantees a man-made Eden.
"My peace I leave you" (John 15:27).

The cross is his final sermon on the mount.
Meek, hungering and thirsting for justice,
peacemaking,
suffering persecution,
he will ascend his pulpit
and stretch himself between earth and heaven
willing to embrace in his extended arms
all who thirst for justice.
"If anyone thirsts, let him come to me,
let him drink who believes in me" (John 7:37–38).

His cross become crucifix become salvation.
Those who desire to change oppression to love,
condemnation to support,
hatred to service,
legalism to rapture
must first nail their own selfishness,
authoritarianism, self-righteousness,
indifference, haughtiness, fear, and security
to the cross.

They must be willing to risk personal crucifixion
to bring Christ's salvation to a society
enslaved in wealth that is careless of the poor,
enslaved in power that is ruthless toward the helpless,
enslaved in lust that is heartless toward the innocent.

15

Once he willingly embraced the cross,
people would never again look at one another with indifference
or treat each other with oppression without the searing pain of guilt.
Through the cross he redeemed us from our sin.

Every sin after that would be
a taunting scream for him
to come down from the cross,
to turn stones into bread,
to cast himself from the Temple's pinnacle,
to build his Kingdom in the factories of our progress
and on the foundation of our runaway technology,
even at the expense of those already
devastated,
exploited,
dehumanized.

There is no easy, sophisticated, clinically sterilized way
to renew the world,
to establish justice,
to bring about peace.
"If anyone wishes to come after me,
let him deny himself,
take up his cross
and follow me" (Matt. 16:24).

Following him means
carrying our cross to our own Golgotha.

Prayer

Jesus, cross-bearer, I fear your way.
There must be a different route. A less strenuous venture.
Your cross contradicts my ease, my comfort, my pleasure, my sloth.
I must be able to work for the betterment of society without having to suffer.

I see you accepting your cross with a willingness
that makes me want to run away, hide with your Apostles —
even, at times, deny you.
Yet I know it is only in your cross that I can find lasting answers to
the legalized depravity,
the wanton destruction,
the organized destitution of our world.

Why is it that when I am confronted with suffering or sacrifice I cringe,
distract myself, find other things more important to do?
Why can I not trust that in taking up my cross you will be with me?
Am I afraid that in having you I will have only your cross?

Help me to see past your cross to your glory
which you also want to share with me.
Help me to come to you, burdened though I may be,
that you may have the opportunity to refresh me on my pilgrimage,
my way of the cross.

Jesus, may your willingness
to carry your cross
be my strength
in losing my life
that I may find it.
(Matt. 10:39).

The Third Station
Jesus Falls the First Time

He falls.
There is no record of anyone helping him up.
"I looked about, but there was no one to help;
I was appalled that there was no one to lend support" (Isa. 63:5).
He lies there, prostrate, beaten, weakened.
It is the moment of decision.
Does he stay down or does he get up and go on?
He struggles to his feet.

The Courage of Jesus

He struggles to his feet.
"Greater love than this no man has
that a man lay down his life for his friends" (John 15:13).
This is his motivation.
This is his courage.
This is not a scenario. It is not a script.
This is brutal reality.
He must struggle to die.
He is determined to go on.
He will do it on his own if he must.
"No one takes my life from me:
I lay it down freely" (John 10:18).

That cross. So unbearably heavy.
The sins of the universe converged in this piece of wood,
the product of advanced technology.

Wood that could be used for a fire, giving warmth,
creating fellowship, fostering security —
all that might bring people together in love, contentment, and belonging.

Wood that could be used to build homes, churches, schools —
any place where people might share concern and care for one another.

Wood that could be used for paper
on which thoughtful sages might pen their sensitive insights,
or gentle poets might carve their prophetic utterances,
or mystical musicians might sing their immortal notes.

Or wood that could be fashioned into a cross — forced into a crucifix,
"...a stumbling block...and an absurdity" (1 Cor. 1:23).

So it is with us.
We can use our technology to grow more food or to crucify human life
while we preserve the structures of our architectural genius.

We can take our technology into the concerns of energy conservation
or we can thrust the industrial spear into the side of our Creator,
draining the last drop of blood and water from our resources.
"Your ancestors ate manna in the desert, but they died" (John 6:49).

No surprise.

When we can plunder and squander
the Son of God,
what can be expected of us
as we rub our greedy hands
over the opulence of his creation?

In the face of all our frustrations,
we watch him get up,
rise from the dust of human oppression,
and move on.
"I can do all things in him who strengthens me" (Phil. 4:13).

Move on.
To even greater oppression.
The greatest.
"Crucify him! Crucify him!" (Luke 23:21).

His courage.
As stark as the cross he carries.
His indomitable will.
Every step toward the place called "The Skull."
Urged on by the force of our sin —
and of his love.
Moving from bad to worse.

Yet his courage is visible.
The courage of a God who promised,
"He will strike at your head,
while you strike at his heel" (Gen. 3:15).

He would share this courage.
Make us fearless.
But we keep looking away.
Looking at others.
Wondering what they may be thinking.
Shrinking from the possible rebukes hurled at us
for daring to be different.
Daring to live the whole gospel.

He would evoke from us some self-respect.
We have so little self-respect
that would merge with his courage.

He would have us get up from
our doubts,
our crises,
our hardships,
our disappointments,
our heartbreaks,
our sin.

Get up and get going.
Following in his steps.

But we are
so weak,
so frightened,
so cowardly.
"Flesh begets flesh, Spirit begets spirit" (John 3:6).

We fear getting up.
We might fall again.
We lack the courage to recognize
that "the just man falls seven times a day" (Prov. 24:16).

Prayer

Jesus, condemned and courageous,
I admit my weakness, my cowardice.
I, like so many others,
do not have the courage to get up from my selfish lifestyle.
It is a way of life that plunders
the wonderful handiwork of our Creator-God.
I, too, hoard and waste,
rape the earth, and pollute the skies.
Courage would force me out of my indifference.
An indifference that makes my life
so comfortable, so secure, so pleasant.

Jesus, your courage prods me on to where I do not want to go.
I do not want to get up and leave my few, almost harmless vices.
Yet you call me onward and upward
to where I shall be stripped of my sloth,
my anger, my lust, my pettiness,
my attachment to familiar ways of sinning.
If I accepted your courage, it might wrench my entire life.

Jesus, may your courage
be my stamina
for getting up
again and again,
realizing that only the weak
fall once.

The Fourth Station
Jesus Meets His Mother

S he is there. His mother.
Almost swallowed up in the jeering mob.
There are a few sympathizers.
But they are silent for the most part.
"To what shall I compare you, O daughter Jerusalem? . . .
For great as the sea is your distress" (Lam. 2:13).
She stands — *Mater dolorosa.*
She peers out at him. He looks at her.
"Who is my mother? Who are my brothers?" (Matt. 12:48).
His eyes are riveted on her.
"Whoever does the will of my heavenly Father . . ." (Matt. 12:50).
His love is infinite. His life is finite.

The Love of Jesus

His love is infinite. His life is finite.

She had said,
"Behold your maidservant.
Be it done to me according to your will" (Luke 1:38).

The will of God for her:
a heart pierced by a sword (Luke 2:35).
And now this.

She is there.
It is the will of her son's father.
No philosophy,
no ideology can explain all this.
Trust.
Firm belief.
"God so loved the world that he sent his only begotten son" (John 3:16).

"All this" was a matter of love.

How different from the love we worry over.
The love we pretend.

We gaze intently on this tableau of selfless love.
And it makes so little sense in the experience of *our* love:
A love
so unappreciative,
so demanding,
so possessive,
so jealous.

A love that measures,
counts,
keeps tabs,
takes turns,
calculates.

A love that
questions,
disbelieves,

suspects,
judges,
condemns.

A love that
sulks,
harbors hurts,
seeks revenge,
plays games,
defames,
and often destroys.

A selfish love.

He stares at her.
His mother.
"There was no room in the inn" (Luke 2:7).

His mother who had caressed him.
Taught him how to talk, to walk, to read, to love.
"Son, why have you done this to us?
You see that your father and I
have been searching for you in sorrow" (Luke 2:48).

She watches him.
Anxiously. No utterance. Memories flood her heart.
"Do not fear, Mary. You have found favor with God" (Luke 1:30).

Like Abraham and Isaac: Mary and Jesus.
She is willing to sacrifice her own son.
"Because you acted as you did
in not withholding from me your beloved son,
I will bless you abundantly" (Gen. 22:16–17).

She has surrendered her son.
He will move on now. Away from her.
She will not withhold him.
"All ages to come shall call me blessed" (Luke 1:48).

It is the will of her son's Father.

"God so loved the world..." (John 3:16).
A world we help to shape.
A world torn and bleeding with the wasted lives of sons and daughters.
The futility of the killings.
The hopelessness of the warring.
A world that tries to buy peace with the bloodmoney of weaponry.
"Nation will rise against nation and kingdom against kingdom" (Luke 21:10).

How deftly we excuse our lack of love. Our indifference.

Survival is a greater value than love, we say.
We do not hate the enemy, just "defend" against him, we say.
We had better get them before they get us, we say.
This will be the war to end all wars. How often will we say that?
"Arms race" and "stockpiling."
Words as commonplace in our everyday conversation
as "please" and "thank you" once were —
when we learned them from our mother.

"Who is my mother?"
We try to understand his love.
A love so sacrificial that even his mother
is drawn — absorbed — into the sacrifice.
A love that suffers. That causes suffering.
So that there may be unity, not walls.
Service, not massacres.
Peace, not warheads,
Justice, not bloated stomachs.

Is it too radical a love for us? Will we fail?
"Crucify him! Crucify him!" (Luke 23:21).

Prayer

Jesus, true love, how can we love one another as you love us
if there is no fundamental justice in our world?
"A new commandment I give you:
that you love one another as I have loved you" (John 15:12).
Yet you are preeminently "the teacher of justice" (Joel 2:23).
Your kingdom of justice and peace is at work right now within our history.
"The kingdom of God is already in your midst" (Luke 17:21).

Our discipleship is to help make that kingdom
more visible, influential, predominant, and all-embracing.
Without our commissioned efforts, there will never be that love
which binds us together in the unity you prayed for and died for.
"That they all may be one as we are" (John 17:22).

Jesus, as I examine my own personal selfishness,
I realize that each denial of love I am responsible for
only subtracts from the universal love of your kingdom.
My selfishness, which seems quite private, in reality contributes
to the plight of peoples who suffer the indignities of injustice.

Help me by the power of your love to be more caring
for those in my immediate circle of family, friends, and associates.
Let our growing concern combine to bring greater love into the world.

May your love,
and that of your mother,
be the spark of our zeal
in the cause of spreading
justice and peace
throughout the human family.

The Fifth Station
Simon Helps Jesus

He needs help.
No one knows this better than the soldiers.
Had they not beaten him?
Didn't one of the more ingenious among them
weave a crown of thorns?
Had they not slammed their reeds against his head
with brutal mockery? (Mark 15:16–19).
"Destroy this temple and in three days I will rebuild it" (John 2:19).
Indeed! He can't even make the short distance to Golgotha!

The Need of Jesus

Indeed! He can't even make the short distance to Golgotha!
The soldiers had their orders.
They were to crucify him.
Not let him drop over dead on the way.
Orders had to be followed.
You don't ask questions.
Don't offer alternatives.
You're not responsible.
You do what you're commanded.
Discipline. That's what counts. Orders are orders.
And they had theirs.
"So Pilate...handed him over to be crucified" (Mark 15:15).

He needs help.
"I am the Vine, you are the branches" (John 15:5).
Yet how often we, like the soldiers, shift our responsibility.

Unlike the soldiers, however, we're not under orders.
It's worse.
We rationalize. We lie to ourselves.
We excuse ourselves from the responsibility for our actions.
Or inaction.

We fabricate.
We have reasonable cover-ups:
For the hostile defenses of our position.
For our lack of involvement.
For our apathy, our lethargy, our squandered energy.
What can I do? We plead.

People in our world are dropping over dead from hunger every day.
"Have you been to the grocery store lately?" we protest.
"It's impossible to put food on the table," we gripe,
as we sit in front of our kitchen-colored TV sets.
"I was hungry and you fed me" (Matt. 25:35).

Political prisoners waste away in the rot of injustice.
"There are too many kooks in the world," we bellow.
"They ought to round them all up, make an example," we whine.
"I was in prison and you visited me" (Matt. 25:36).

32

He needs help.
The soldiers don't pick
someone from the crowd.
They pick Simon.
"...coming in from the fields" (Mark 15:21).

In from the fields.
Where there is life and growth and hope.
Where the future breaks forth in green shoots
and the past has been ploughed into furrows.
Where the present is wheat and weeds growing together.
Where divine patience and human endeavor
will not judge until the harvest (Matt. 13:24–30).

In from the fields to the city.
The center of commerce.
The seat of government.
The pride of civilization.

And here Forgiveness has been condemned.
Here Love is being put to death.

The soldiers "pressed Simon into service to carry the cross" (Mark 15:21).

Maybe they thought Simon wouldn't know about Pilate.
"What crime has he committed?" (Mark 15:14).
"I find no case against him" (John 19:6).

Maybe they hoped Simon would assume
Jesus was just another criminal,
legally condemned to capital punishment.
Just another thug.

Simon had been out in the fields.
He couldn't know how the religious leaders chose death over Life:
forcing Pilate to "release Barabbas" (Mark 15:11).

It had been such an obvious miscarriage of justice.
A mad mob scene.
But orders are orders.

So they pressed Simon into service.
"You have not chosen me: I have chosen you" (John 15:16).

How often do we have to be "pressed into service"?
In our families.
Our parishes.
Our communities.

"From his riches we have all received,
grace for grace" (John 1:16).
Riches we hoard.
We refuse to share.
"My job is to save my own soul," we argue.
Injustices are the problems of the leaders.

"The bureaucracy's to blame," we rationalize.
Why volunteer?
World worries are beyond our efforts.
No one person can bear the concerns of all
unless it be God Himself.
Why carry a larger, heavier cross?
Let the Lord do it.
It's just not my responsibility.
We excuse.

Prayer

O Jesus, Jesus, Jesus. Forgive my irresponsibility. Forgive my excuses.
My transparent, self-serving excuses. Forgive.

You need help. You need me...
to continue your work of justice, liberation, truth, peace, reconciliation.
You need me, that in my flesh I may "fill up what's lacking
in the sufferings of Christ for the sake of his body" (Col. 1:24).

The Vine. That's what you called yourself.
The Vine who gives life to us, the branches. Who grows us, the branches.
Who infuses power into us, the branches.
"I am the Vine, you are the branches" (John 15:5).
You need us. Depend on us.
The vine needs the branches to bear the fruit.
"The man who has faith in me will do the works I do
and far greater ones than these" (John 14:12).

I intensify my faith that I might fulfill your need.
I want to be a productive branch — drawing all my strength from you —
bringing forth the fresh fruits of justice and peace.
Fresh fruits to be harvested and consumed
by those who otherwise dine on the fast foods of expediency and indifference.
The frozen foods of malice and bigotry.
The canned foods of self-containment and procrastination.

*May your need for us motivate us
to cooperative and fruitful efforts
so that your triumphant inventory
may prove valid in us:
"I entrusted to them
the message you entrusted to me
and they received it" (John 17:8).*

35

The Sixth Station
Veronica Wipes Jesus' Face

S he steps forward.
   Bright dreams now faded into disappointed hope
   etch lines of hesitancy around her eyes. Veronica.
No one stops her.
A towel. A face. Blood, dirt, sweat.
"...your face will never be ashamed" (Ps. 34:6).
An imprint. A sharing.
As always, nothing is offered him that is not returned a hundredfold,
"Behold we have left all things..." (Mark 10:28).
He shares. He always does.

The Sharing of Jesus

He shares. He always does.

Later his disciples would say,
"Silver and gold I have not,
but what I have I give to you" (Acts 3:6).
Silver and gold — so convenient.
He had shared:
his teaching,
his power,
his healing,
his compassion,
his forgiveness,
his tears,
his amazement,
his fear.

And now,
through his death,
his Spirit.

"If I fail to go,
the Paraclete will never come to you" (John 16:7).

There would be no forgetting.
The imprint would remain to remind.
Try as we might to forget.
At least not to remember.
Tragedies.
How earnestly we want them behind us.

Like Pilate.
"He called for water and washed his hands" (Matt. 27:24).
Officially irresponsible
and "...innocent of the blood of this just man" (Matt. 27:24).

Pilate would wash Jesus
out of his life.
Nothing to remind him.
To haunt him.
"This just man."

Was it for effect?
A final irony.
An imperial attempt
to humiliate the chief priests
in their angry jealousy (Mark 15:10).
After all,
it was they who had taunted,
"We have no king but Caesar" (John 19:15).
So be it.
"Take him and crucify him yourselves" (John 19:6).

A sacrilegious moment.
Government and institutional religion bound in alliance.
And its name was "civil religion."
From that moment on the true followers of Jesus would have to oppose
every form of civil religion.

Discipleship would forever mean
resistance to any government
that would oppress and dehumanize,
exploit and enslave
for its own dictatorial power
or dishonest economic growth
or unjust territorial acquisition.
Even more.
Genuine Christians would have to witness
against any church that wedded itself
to such a government in the nuptials of civil religion.

This they would do by sharing as he had shared.
Proclaiming as he had proclaimed.
Protesting as he had protested.
"If you free this man, you are no 'Friend of Caesar'" (John 19:12).

No friends of Caesar,
they would sacrifice their lives as he had.
Subversives,
they would imprint their Christ-identity on the fabric of history.
"That day saw the beginning
of a great persecution in the church..." (Acts 8:1).

Jesus shared.
And we, his church, can never forget.
Never enter into an alliance
that even passively allows governments
to thwart the development of peoples.
To secure an abundance
while others languish in destitution.

"Once there was ... a beggar named Lazarus
who ... longed to eat the scraps that
fell from the rich man's table" (Luke 16:19–21).

Jesus confirms his imprint on us.
Sacramentally.
To bury our heads in the sands of parochial affairs,
pretending that manipulative governments
and exploitative multinationals
don't make a difference is like
"a sow [that] bathes by wallowing in the mire" (2 Pet. 2:22).

To rest satisfied with me-and-my-God religion
is to close praying hands into the clenched fists of selfishness.
A distortion of his imprint.

Jesus shares.
Today.
In and through us.
His branches.
His concern: the sins of the world.
Our concern: the Lamb who takes them away.
His imprint, destined for the renewal of the face of the earth.
Can we risk the complacency of an immediately gratifying I-thou sharing?

Prayer

Jesus, as your church, we are positioned within society as its critical conscience.
Yet we are afraid.
Civil religion has a way of making sinful institutions
appear as the new salvation of the world.
To be critical is to invite
the displeasure, the scorn, the persecution of the powerful, of our loved ones.
Rebels, ingrates, fanatics, malcontents. That's what we'd be called.
Yet the cross was the punishment for insurrectionists.
He maintains that he himself is Christ, a King (Luke 23:2).

To share as you shared means
to be the critic of a society that would pretend to divinity.
A society where technocrats are the new high priests.
Where unbridled scientific progress is the new ritual.
Where economic tyranny is the new body and blood of sacrifice.

Help me to share by making life a Eucharist.
A breaking. A pouring out.
A breaking of my selfishness, my pride, my fear, my hostility, my injustice.
A pouring out of my love, my concern, my hope,
my compassion, my peace, my problem-solving criticism.

May your sharing
make me become
what I receive:
a holy communion.

41

The Seventh Station
Jesus Falls the Second Time

He falls again.
"My food is to do the will of him who sent me" (John 4:34).
His perfection is his father's will.
Even if it means this humiliation. This degradation.
The cosmic Lord plunging into the dust
of this tiny particle of his vast creation.
Barely able to concentrate.
Pain.
The crashing pain of universal sin
scattered throughout every cell of his divinely sensitized body.
Humiliation. Degradation.

The Perfection of Jesus

43

Humiliation. Degradation.
His memory slips back.

A painful day.
They had approached him.
Thrown her to the ground.
"Teacher, this woman has been caught in the act of adultery" (John 8:4).
There she was.
In the dust of public accusation.
Condemned.
"In the law Moses ordered such a woman to be stoned" (John 8:5).

We fall.
If addicted to
perfectionism —
which looks to appearances as the Supreme Court —
we are embarrassed beyond words.

Even words of repentance.
We bow our heads in anguished humiliation.
Our world collapses.
We want to stay down.
Never rise again.
Our mood is desperation.
Its name is "Abyss."
We have no hope.
There is no God who can forgive.
"Let the little children come to me" (Matt. 19:14).

Our pride-in-virtue has robbed us of childlike trust.
Virtue has been self-canonization.
Love, a duty.
Sacrifice, an obligation.
We stockpiled our merits ever so carefully.
Measured our piety against the law ever so meticulously.

Perfectionism.
"Teacher, who has sinned, this man or his parents?" (John 9:2).
Confidently virtuous, we righteously pointed our finger at the sinner.
We asked, "Who has sinned?"

Fortified by our own holiness,
we had no fear of retaliation.
"Has no one condemned you?
Neither will I" (John 8:10–11).

Perfectionism.
Another legalistic distortion.
"Be perfect
as your heavenly Father
is perfect" (Matt. 5:48).

Perfection.
Flexible, exuberant, creative, joyous.
Always a sinner, yet always being saved.
Always in communion with other sinners.
Sharing universal salvation.
Perfection out of admitted sin.
Repented sin.
Perfection out of sympathy for those who fall
and ask help to rise again.

Perfectionism.
Said the accused:
If your words of correction had been filled with pain,
I would have knelt and asked your absolution.
Filled as they were with self-righteous insensitivity for my weaknesses,
I could only stand and beg God
to deliver me from those who
thank him that they are not like the rest (Luke 18:11).

Perfection.
Steeped in love.

Perfectionism.
Rooted in legalism.

The letter of the law for its own sake.
Shorn of empathy, understanding, forgiveness.
Applied to ourselves, it becomes scrupulosity.
To others, self-righteous judgment.

Perfectionists.
They who know what's best for everyone else.
Their specific prayer format or their particular religious experience
becomes the "only way."
They who erect a fortress out of traditions (with a small "t")
from which they hurl their interdicts and anathemas.
"How can wedding guests go in mourning
so long as the groom is with them?" (Matt. 9:15).

Perfection.
Generous and concerned.

Perfectionism.
Selfish and self-centered.
Blind to the injustices that torture the captives of greed to death.
Deaf to the pleas of today's holy innocents
— men, women, and children —
twisting and twitching
in the dry martyrdom of conscience-violating manipulation.
"And who is my neighbor?" (Luke 10:29).

He gets up.
Again.
"The kingdom of God is not meat and drink
but peace and justice and joy in the Holy Spirit" (Rom. 14:17).
Peace, justice, joy.
His food, his father's will. His perfection.

Perfection is getting up, again and again.
Moving forward.
Inching along.
Sharing salvation.
"But a certain Samaritan came upon him..." (Luke 10:33).

Prayer

Jesus, fallen yet rising, my vanity turns perfection into perfectionism.
Paralyzes my knee so that it cannot bend at your name (Phil. 2:10).
Perfectionism is the most subtle, if not insidious, form of vanity.
My perfectionism, to whatever degree,
makes me believe I am more than what I am.
Perfection tells me that I am much less than what I can become.

Help me to use my falls to develop humility.
A humility that places me at the total service of others.
That prompts me to see others as superior to me
because of their needs (Phil. 2:3).
A humility that is a warm embrace of the weaknesses and limitations
of all those who need support in the struggle to rise again.
To move on toward perfection even if it means suffering.
Even crucifixion.
And death to
my perfectionism.

May your perfection
be my urgent humility.

The Eighth Station
Jesus Comforts the Women

Weeping.
Was it really?
Some women.
With their children. Weeping.
He stopped.
"There was following Jesus a great crowd of people
and among them were some women
who were bewailing and lamenting him" (Luke 23:27).
Even in his agony, he would find words for others.

The Compassion of Jesus

Even in his agony, he would find words for others.
Standing before Pilate he had "no further response" (Mark 15:5).
Now others were suffering.
They needed consolation.
He would share his limitless compassion.
"We have nothing here but five loaves and two fish" (Matt. 14:17).

Their tears.
A nonviolent protest.
A witness against a barbarism disguised as defense against attack.
After all, he had attacked:
the moneychangers (John 2:15),
the Pharisees (Matt. 7).

He speaks.
"Daughters of Jerusalem,
weep not for me
but for yourselves and for your children" (Luke 23:28).

Once before mothers had wept.
Had wailed.
Herod's "ordered massacre" (Matt. 2:16).

Today, women actually offer their children to the butcher's knife.

Then,
Herod had been afraid, had acted out of political expediency.
Now,
doctors establish chain store abortion clinics, acting out of greed.
Do they ever weep? These doctors. These judges. These women.

It's rather easy to kill what we don't see.
A fetus we call "it."
Unnamed.
Unheld.
Unwanted.

It can all be done with the driest eyes.
Steely eyes.
Focused like spikes as sharp and unfeeling as a death-dealing scalpel.

Clinical precision.
Professional detachment.
Judicial approval.
Maternal convenience.

Just a little mess to be cleaned up.
Just an "it" — this human being.

"Weep...for your children."
How many mothers have wept since?

Tears that sent their children off to war.

Tears that read the telegrams:
Missing in action.
Killed in action.

Tears that visit the living dead in veterans' hospitals
forgotten by all but a few still-bewildered loved ones.

Will the tears never stop?
Gold Star mothers still meet,
still weep
quiet but unforgetting tears.

It's rather easy to absorb 10,000 lives here or 100,000 lives there.
Numbers benumb.
If we were to concentrate through a mother's heart
on just one human being....
All the love invested.
All the care given.
All the education afforded.
All the dreams vanished.
All this potential unrealized.

One precious, unique human being.
Lying dead.
The horror.
The repulsive ugliness.
Bearable only as a cross.

The more we kill, the more we become suicidal.
We keep killing the human race. On battlefields. In clinics. In courts.

Jesus had wept.
Bitter tears of compassion.
Over Jerusalem. Over its rejection.
"He wept over it and said,
if only you had known the path to peace ... " (Luke 19:41–42).
Now he suffers for all the Jerusalems throughout history.
Where the wealthy, the powerful, the ruthless
continue to reject him in the poor, the wasted, the martyred.

His compassion penetrates all the Jerusalems where mothers weep.
Weep over children who sit in marble silence like rows of tombstones.
Over children dying of curable diseases for which there is no medicine.
Over children who are not even aware of the scraps falling from the tables
of landowners with their "bigger and better barns."
Of industrialists with their "new wine in old wineskins."
Of dictators with their hoarded "coin of the realm."
"If they were to keep silence,
I tell you the very stones would cry out" (Luke 19:40).

Through us, the members of his Body, he would share his compassion.
But we are indifferent.
The suffering masses are so far removed.
And when they come close?
Well, we have our own problems.
"I can *donate* something," we say.
Compassion takes time. Effort.

Prayer

Jesus, overflowing with compassion, how many misplaced tears have I shed.
Over broken dreams. Because everything doesn't go my way.
Because I can't dangle God on a string. Can't bribe.

Even when I attempt to be compassionate,
I confine myself to the faraway physically oppressed and economically poor.
I exclude those who are spiritually impoverished or morally bankrupt.
I exclude those I dislike, those who oppose me,
those who deceive, those who are moralistic dictators.
I exclude the emotionally oppressed, the intellectually poor.
Those trapped in immaturity. Imprisoned in neurosis.
Those who are simply different.

"O Lord, hear my prayer and let my cry come unto you" (Ps. 102:2).
Jesus, help me to be blessed by mourning for all the pain in the world
that I may be a comfort with my compassion.
Let me reach out to each suffering person
through my prayer, my penance, my mortification.

May your compassion
be the tears
of my concern.

The Ninth Station
Jesus Falls the Third Time

He falls again.
Such a short distance from his last fall.
Pain is now torture.
This fall. It seems so final.
"...all the kingdoms of the world...I will bestow on you
if you prostrate yourself in homage before me" (Matt. 4:8–9).
He would not. He did not. He had his mission:
His Father's Kingdom...of peace and unity, of justice and love.

He lies there.
His mission flashes before him.

The Mission of Jesus

His mission flashes before him.
In the synagogue.
A lifetime ago.
"He has sent me to bring glad tidings to the poor,
to proclaim liberty to captives,
recovery of sight to the blind
and release to prisoners" (Luke 4:18).

The cross.
Pinning him to the ground.
An essential part of his mission.
Had he not identified himself with
the poor,
the suffering,
the sick,
the possessed,
the outcast,
"the least of my brethren"? (Matt. 25:40).

The cross seals this identification.
"They shall not die
and go down to the Pit" (Isa. 51:14).

He was not the Baptist.
He had left the wilderness.
Had pursued his mission in cities and hamlets.
Had gone into
homes,
synagogues,
the temple,
vineyards,
wheat fields,
sheepfolds.

People had crowded him.
A crush of desperate humanity.
"If only I can touch his cloak..." (Matt. 9:21).

He had entered into life fully.
Yet always confronted.

Ultimately rejected.
Like the Baptist.

The most heartbreaking
disillusionment of all:
the veiled hatred of
right-thinking,
law-abiding,
God-fearing
churchgoers.

"John the Baptist came
neither eating bread, nor drinking wine
and you say,
'He is mad!'

"The Son of Man came
and he both ate and drank
and you say,
'Here is a glutton and a drunkard,
a friend of tax collectors and sinners'" (Luke 7:33–34).
We have a phrase. A no-win situation.

His mission.
In the peaceful hillsides of Galilee.
In the turbulent streets of Jerusalem.
For him the world was never a prison. Never an exile.
Not for him the mystics' fierce ascent to God. Ignoring the world.
He had embraced the world. In all its sinfulness.
In the lilies of the field. The birds of the air (Luke 12:27, 24).

Now, in the intense suffering the world could inflict,
he would love the world into redemption.
For him religion had never been separate from life.
We watch him lying there.
Carrying out his mission.

Yet, unlike him, do we not use our religion, often, as an unconscious escape?
Religion is out there, somewhere we can go
to get away . . . from life.

From unadmitted defenses. From unresolved guilt feelings.
From religious immaturity. From a lack of personal development.
From a poor self-image. From anxious routines.
From despondency. From insecurity. From a love gone sour.
Escape from people who agitate. Who use.
Who hurt. Who are indifferent.

Too often, do we not use religion?
As a hideaway where we don't have to face ourselves honestly!
Our problems creatively.
As a tranquilizer for our deep-seated emotional problems.
As a glue for our unintegrated personalities.
As a Band-Aid for the gaping wounds in our character.
As a security blanket for our fears.
As a compartment separate from life.

We pray for strength.
What we really want is for God to wave a magic wand.
The more religion becomes an escape,
the more it can become a superstition.
Tragically, religion as escape
reinforces the very problems we are trying to run from, to deny.
Our mission is to the world (Matt. 28:19)
in all its potential for peace, for justice, for community.
Yet religion as escape degenerates into neutrality
on the pressing moral and social issues of our day.
A safe neutrality.
Even a sanctimonious neutrality.
A neutrality that lends support to sinful social structures — by default.

He gets up again.
Carrying the cross is not passive resignation.
Carrying the cross is seizing the problem, working through it.
Perhaps it's a lack of communication.
Carrying the cross is the suffering experienced
in trying to speak again in self-revelation.
Suffering is often intensified by the other's refusal to cooperate.
Carrying the cross means repeated efforts.
Getting up many times. Even though we suffer.
Carrying the cross is seizing life, in its totality, as our mission.

Prayer

Jesus, you share your mission with me.
Yet for me to fulfill this mission, religion must be an integrating force in my life.
The problem is that my escapism forces a wedge between religion and life.
I want religion to be a profusion of problem-solving miracles.
I want the consolations of God, not the God of consolations.

I use religion as an escape from carrying the cross —
the very center and source of mission.
And even when I do get involved,
I don't want the suffering of confrontation or misunderstanding.
I seek peace in an escape from the bruising realities of life
which I must enter into fully if I am to be
the bearer of glad tidings to the world.

Help me to understand that grace builds on nature.
That I must develop my psychological capacities for spiritual awareness.
Help me to realize that holiness is wholeness.
That to practice religion authentically, I must be healthy emotionally.

May the fulfillment
of your mission
be my determination
to get up and carry
this cross of mine.

The Tenth Station
Jesus Is Stripped

He has arrived.
Finally.
Torturously.
They strip him.
What is it about love that it can be so intensely hated?
"Play the prophet, which one struck you?" (Luke 22:64).
That was it!
In their simplistic ridicule
they had unwittingly affirmed his role.
He was indeed a prophet. He stands stripped.
No heralding angels. No worshiping magi. No shining star.

The Prophecy of Jesus

No heralding angels. No worshiping magi. No shining star.
Only the prophet.
Stripped of all human rights.
Of all dignity.
Of all consolation.
All support.
Naked.
Abandoned.

Alone.

"You are trying to kill me, a man who has told you the truth" (John 8:40).
He had dared to put into words
what he had heard from his Father (John 15:15).
"You have heard it said.... But I say to you..." (Matt. 5:21–22).

He had dared to speak the truth.
"When you pray, do not behave like the hypocrites" (Matt. 6:5).

Truth they didn't want to hear, to face:
"Tax collectors and prostitutes
are entering the kingdom of God before you" (Matt. 21:31).

Truth that required change.
"Unless you change and become like little children..." (Matt. 18:3).
Change
in their beliefs,
in their worldview,
in their lives.
"A great prophet has risen among us" (Luke 7:16).

His truth has threatened them,
stripped them.
So they projected their hatred onto him.
Love, unclothed, can be so intensely hated.

Prophets are like that.
They disturb.
Question our nostalgia for a more virtuous past.
Ask us to rethink traditional definitions.

Offer new insights
that threaten old securities.
Make us face the aching problems
of our cultural heritage.
Keep jolting us
with the radical moral teachings
of the gospel.

To this very hour
we don't want these prophets around.
They talk about consumerism.
Call it selfish.
Remind us of the starving masses discarded on the trash heap of life.
Urge us not to live beyond our needs.
Attack the "new" which advertising offers as a snob value.
Ask why we live in a twelve-room house if six rooms are sufficient.

Prophets talk about justice.
Ask why we work for institutions that treat the poverty-stricken
as throwaway props only to amass corporate profits.
Cry out against the unequal distribution of resources.
The rich getting richer.
The poor, poorer.

They condemn our power equations
with brazen regimes
that run roughshod over the defenseless.

They accost the false patriotism
that compromises the gospel ideal of the kingdom
for the sake of big government.

The false economic loyalty
which sells out the gospel counsel of poverty
to big business.

Prophets are like that.
They really do tell it like it is:
Deliberate termination of a pregnancy is murder.
Defense build-up is preparation for war.

63

Wanton waste of tax money is theft.
Reinforcing poverty and destitution is avarice.
Runaway technology is vanity.
Worship without forgiveness is self-righteousness.
Prayer without service is selfishness.
The practice of virtue without compassion is pride.
"They persecuted the prophets before you" (Matt. 5:12).

Who wants to hear all this?
We have a right to a comfortable way of life.
Who needs these prophets? These reminders? This tension?
Who needs radical conversion?
Most certainly the gospel demands more than the letter of the law.
A total commitment.
But do we have to strip ourselves of every last garment?
Live in stark detachment?
How many stomachs would that fill?
How many unjust governments would that bring to the knees of reform?

So we dismiss the prophets.
Call them "prophets of doom."
Lifeless, humorless, joyless antagonists.
Tense, inflexible, unrelenting fanatics.
"Let well enough alone," we say.
These prophets. How do we know that they're not just off on an ego trip?
Overcompensating for some past guilt?
"Then they crucified him and divided up his garments" (Mark 15:24).

Prayer

Jesus, true prophet, stripped of what little you had of this world's goods,
we have been baptized into your prophetic power.
Far from ignoring or even persecuting the prophets,
we should *be* those prophets, your prophets.

But to be your prophet I must have a clear vision,
unobstructed by the blinding glitter of my possessions.
I don't have to live in deprivation or in agonizing insecurity.
But I must practice holy indifference —
if I am to be your prophetic voice.
A holy indifference that says: If I have something, fine.
If I don't, just as fine.
Help me so that whatever possessions I have,
if I should lose them, I would be content.

Lead me in the practice of holy indifference
that will never allow my possessions to dim my eyes
to the harsh focus of world misery.
A holy indifference which will make me realize
that it is what I am, not what I have, that has eternal value.
That it is what I can become, not what I can acquire more of,
that will give my involvement a redeeming timeliness.

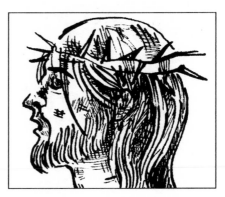

May your prophetic power
be my openness to our Father's
"call for the victory of justice"
(Isa. 45:8).

The Eleventh Station
Jesus Is Crucified

They attack him with metallic savagery.
The hammer. The nails.
Condemned in his innocence, he is crucified in his love.
They stretch him out. On the paten of the cross.
"My hour has not yet come" (John 2:4).
His hour is not to be cheated. It is now. It is total sacrifice.
An offering as intense as it is cosmic.
The Word that spoke the universe is now the Word of consecration.

The Sacrifice of Jesus

The Word that spoke the universe is now the Word of consecration.

Golgotha.
The altar.

Here he is priest.
What he is, he gives.
"I have greatly desired to eat this Passover with you" (Luke 22:15).
He had promised his body.
As food.
His blood.
As drink (John 6:53).
He had offered himself. As bread. As wine (Matt. 26:26–28).

Golgotha.
The altar.

Here he is victim.
"Let his blood be on us and on our children" (Matt. 27:25).
He had said it plainly.
He would be a victim.
Handed over.
Condemned.
Mocked.
Spit upon.
Flogged.
And finally killed (Mark 10:33–34).

The victim who would lay down his life of his own accord.
Freely (John 10:18).
Out of love (John 15:13).
We contemplate this scene.
Anointed into his priesthood.
In baptism.
Will we share in his victimhood?
"This is my blood . . . to be poured out . . . " (Matt. 26:28).
"Can you drink the cup I drink?" (Mark 10:38).

Unless we absorb his victimhood,
his sacrifice will remain out there.

On the altar.
The pageant. The drama.
We will be spectators.
Not victims with him.
"Not everyone who says,
'Lord, Lord' shall enter
the kingdom of heaven..." (Matt. 7:21).

Ours will be adopted holy thoughts.
Prayer locked into routine.
Words sent skyward while we stay comfortably fastened
to the habits of our undisturbed, unchanged lifestyle.
"This people pay me lip service
but their heart is far from me" (Mark 7:6).

We eat him.
Our sacrifice.
He transforms us.
Into himself.
But he is both priest and victim.

In our priesthood we consecrate the human race.
In our victimhood we swallow the sacrifices of a tortured world.
People so lonely in their search for happiness.
People too hungry to even think of love.
Too tired to cry.
Too gaunt to smile.
Too desperate to extend a beseeching hand.
Too old before they're young.
Too frightened to live — all over the tortured world.

If we refuse to internalize his sacrifice,
can we grasp the hand next to us and utter, "Peace"?
Can we?

When we refuse to touch our own pain.
When we recoil from theirs.
Next to us.
An old person flickering and guttering like a sanctuary candle.
The young person singing sin. Laughing pressure. Effervescing dreams.

The wife waiting for her husband to return,
to eat, to snore, to shave, to leave again.
The husband flopped on an easy chair
fantasizing successes as worn as the slipcover that hides the holes.
Can we?

When the victim remains on the altar.
"I just don't get anything out of the Mass," we complain.
We who share in the priesthood of Christ — all of us.
They nail him to the cross.
Stretched out, he stretches us beyond ourselves.
Into his glory and power.
But we must first be nailed.

Nails. As much a part of life as is the Spirit.
Yet we want the exuberance of the Spirit too quickly.
The soothing performance of a victimless priesthood too easily.
The glorified wounds of resurrection joy too effortlessly.
And all without the nails.
Without the nails there can be no release of the Spirit's power in our lives.
The nails tell us that dying is the prelude to rising.
Crucifixion precedes resurrection.
Death is the context of new life.
Struggle comes before affirmation.
Openness to the new is the condition for growth and fulfillment.

Realism is the seedground for idealism.
"Whoever would preserve his life
will lose it..." (Mark 8:35), the nails remind us.
Nails that pierce our lives.
Fasten us to our sacrifices.
Nails that make us victims with him.
On the altar.
In our hearts.
In our lifestyles.

Prayer

Jesus, I go to Mass. I am satisfied with the change on the altar,
the bread and wine into your body and blood.
I am not particularly interested in any other change.
Why is it that there are those who insist
that the Eucharist must mean a transformation of my lifestyle?
Is my Mass any less pious if I prefer my serene, private life
to the public tumult of social action for justice and peace?

I think I know the answers. The Eucharist is sharing.
The Eucharist proclaims sacrifice
so that everyone will have equal access to all resources.
I cannot enter into your life-giving death without dying to myself,
my comfort, my self-centeredness, my private piety.
If your sacrifice is to become mine,
the Eucharist cannot be isolated from the rest of my life.

I cannot fill myself with you, the Bread of Life, and continue to ignore
those who hunger because of my lifestyle of selfish consumerism.
I cannot eat your Eucharistic body
and refuse to swallow your Mystical Body
with its insistent and painful disruption of my middle-class security,
my comfortable piety, my Mass.

*May the nails of your crucifixion
make the Eucharist
my personal, internalized sacrifice
on behalf of those who hunger
and thirst for justice.*

The Twelfth Station
Jesus Dies

He hangs there on the cross.
"Philip, he who sees me sees the Father" (John 14:9).
The closeness. The intimacy. The oneness.
"The Father knows me and I know the Father" (John 10:15).
"All that the Father has belongs to me" (John 16:15).
"The Father and I are one" (John 10:30).
"I can never be alone; the Father is with me" (John 16:32).
The union of purest mysticism.
We are never alone. God is always God-with-us.

The Mysticism of Jesus

We are never alone. God is always God-with-us.
What is God really like?
We wonder.
We question.

Does he honestly care?
How great is his love?
Is he truly good?

For answers we only have to gaze at the crucifixion scene.
Seeing Jesus, we see the Father.
And we know God!

No words needed.
Or concepts.
Or definitions.
Only the crucifix.
To know God.
And his infinite love.

He hangs there.
On the cross.
"My God, my God, why have you forsaken me?" (Mark 15:34).
"Never alone"?
The darkness that covers the earth
has penetrated the very depths of his being.
The dark night of the soul.
The mystical experience of abandonment.

The more intimately we enter into God, the more he purifies us.
From attachments.
From sin.
From ourselves.

Mystical purification.
But he "who did not know sin" (2 Cor. 5:21)
could hardly be purified from it.
The one final experience that could be taken from him:
the consolation of God.
God "made him to be sin" (2 Cor. 5:21).

Hanging there he was experiencing
the unbearable horror
of all sin throughout the ages.
He felt the isolation,
the alienation,
the loneliness that is sin.

Pierced by the holiness of God so searingly
that the slightest fault assumed the horrendous proportion of all sin.
From Adam to the coming of the Son of Man on the clouds (Matt. 24:30).
The terrorizing pain of mysticism.

Mystical prayer.
A gift from God.
Yet not reserved for the chosen few.
As grace is the beginning of glory, so faith is the initiation into mysticism.

And we can prepare for this gift by a more creative awareness in faith.

But false humility protests against mystical experience.
We know the gift can be ours.
We settle for saying prayers instead of praying.
To struggle through prayer to God is to struggle in prayer.
Serious efforts at praying can result in pain, desolation, and abandonment.
We recoil.

Mysticism can mean no warmth.
No feeling of intimacy.
No consolation.
Nothing but emptiness.
The cry of being forsaken.

There are moments in prayer
where joy stretches into the outermost reaches of ecstasy.
And there are times when prayer itself can be sheer torture.
Utter agony.
When the pain hovers on the edges of despair.

Not the despair of hopelessness.
But of human limitation.

We can receive so little of God when his totality is our only consuming desire.
His death releases his Spirit.
His Spirit will lead us to the heights and depths of mystical experience —
if we are willing.

To follow his Spirit we must die to ourselves (John 12:24).
We must lose our lives (Matt. 10:39).
And it is this "dying," this "losing," that strikes terror in our hearts.

At first, so exciting.
But as the last breaths of this dying to self come closer,
we are filled with dread.
Dread that in losing ourselves we will have nothing else, except God.

He hangs there.
On the cross.
"There shall be lamentation when I pass through you" (Amos 5:17).
He passes into the center of his being.
Passes through his center into God.
Ultimate mysticism.

So completely, totally, absolutely
that his "passing through" is the final surrender of his life.
The mystical and the physical merge.
"Father, into your hands I commend my spirit" (Luke 23:46).
The union of purest mysticism.

Prayer

Through you, Jesus, your Father passes into me,
with his redeeming love, his saving power, which I must share.
Mystical prayer is the total dying to myself
that only selfless, loving service might remain.
A mystical death so complete
that my concern for others might become universal.

An "emptying out" of self so absolute that there might be unlimited room
for the suffering, anguish, hunger, and oppression of the whole world.
Mystical prayer is the lance piercing my heart to receive all who are in need.

Jesus, you share with me the mystical love of your Father, your Spirit, yourself.
Dwelling within me. Closer to me than I am to myself.
As you, in mystical love, experienced the full impact
of all the sinfulness of history,
so I must allow into my life the injustices, poverty, absence of peace,
hatred, bigotry, selfishness, both individual and worldwide,
of my current history.

In mystical openness I, like you,
must give my life "as a ransom for many" (Matt. 20:28)
through my sacrifices, my mortifications, my sufferings,
humiliations, inadequacies, doubts, prayer, action.

*May your mysticism
be my redeeming,
self-sacrificing embrace
of a world that
"groans and is in agony
even until now"
(Rom. 8:22).*

The Thirteenth Station
Jesus Is Taken Down
from the Cross

His suffering is over now.
He is at peace.
The chalice has passed.
But only after it had been drained.
His limp body rests on her lap.
"Woman, how does this concern of yours involve me?"
he had asked at Cana (John 2:4).
She had not been puzzled. Or deterred.
No argument. No altercation.
"Do whatever he tells you" (John 2:5).
She is always there.

The Peace of Jesus

She is always there.
Always there. Always involved. Even to this:
"Near the cross of Jesus there stood his mother" (John 19:25).
Her concern would now be universal.
"Woman, there is your son" (John 19:26).
She held his dead body.
For her, now, a new body.
His Mystical Body.

Not without grief would she be mother to this new body.
Immaculately conceived.
Originally sinless.
She had suffered.
Bloodlessly wounded. Internally crucified.
The sword had pierced her heart (Luke 2:35).

The thoughts of many hearts of a happier life.
Cynical thoughts about the future.
Desperate thoughts about a fulfilling love.
Sorrowful thoughts.
Judgmental thoughts.
Hateful thoughts.

She held him as only a mother could.
His suffering was over now.
He was at peace.
One day he would be called "Prince of Peace."

For now?
Far off in imperial Rome?
Just another of those fanatical,
troublemaking itinerant preachers.
The provinces were filled with them!

This province though.
Always that talk about a one, true god.
Yahweh they called him. Ridiculous.
Well, as long as the governor
could get these religious zealots on some trumped-up charge,
then peace — the *Pax Romana* — would reign.

What was this one's name?
Joshua or Jesus or Jethro or something?
The people would eventually forget.
They always do.

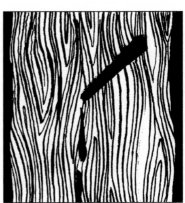

But they didn't forget.
"Within a short time
you will lose sight of me,
but soon after that
you will see me again" (John 16:16).

"Father, forgive them..." (Luke 23:34).
One of his final prayers.
A prayer for reconciliation, for peace.
There can be no peace without reconciliation.
No reconciliation without forgiveness.

"How happy the peacemakers..."
he had exclaimed on the Mount (Matt. 5:9).

His followers would bring his message of peace
into a world that thrived on strife.
On terror.
On war.
And they would suffer for their message.
"I tell you all this so that in me you may find peace.
In the world you will suffer" (John 16:33).

The world hasn't changed much since he said that.
Today terrorists are an intense articulation of our universal context of fear.
The balance of power which, in doublespeak, is used to preserve "peace"
is in reality the balance of terror.
This balance of terror is the peace the world gives.
"My peace is my gift to you;
I do not give it as the world gives peace" (John 14:27).

The peace of Christ will not be found in any balance of terror.
As Christ's followers, as his peacemakers, should we not:
Constantly question the economic manipulations of the peace the world gives?
Continually strive to make others, especially the powerful and influential,

conscious of a false peace which is in fact only the absence of war?
Steadfastly sound the alarm against what at any moment
can go up in mushrooming nuclear smoke?

Our lack of peace can be traced back to our original failure
to understand and live God's initial mandate:
"Take dominion...," his Father had commissioned (Gen. 1:28).

Not the dominion of power:
plundering,
victimizing,
annexing,
exterminating.

Not the dominion of greed:
devastating,
scarring,
hoarding,
wasting.
All preparations for total annihilation.

But the dominion of fruitfulness (Gen. 1:28):
building community,
sharing resources,
caring for the needy,
welcoming the alienated,
forgiving wrongdoers,
understanding those who differ from and with us,
rectifying injustices,
doing to others as we would have them do to us (Matt. 7:12),
and loving one another with a Christ-love (John 15:12).
The dominion of peace.

Prayer

Jesus, of all the farewell gifts you might have given us, you chose peace.
"Peace is my farewell to you, my peace is my gift to you" (John 14:27).
This you said to your disciples shortly before you were arrested.
And even in their panic and fright when they thought they were seeing a ghost,
you had only one word for them, "Peace" (Luke 24:36–37).

There can be no doubt of the priority you give to peace.
There can be no doubt either that,
while I embark on my peacemaking efforts,
I had better be striving to be at peace: with myself, with others.

I am not so zealous a peacemaker as I should be
because I am so filled with interior turmoil:
the unrest of jealousy, the agitation for vengeance,
the anxiety about possessions, the commotion over change,
the internal eruptions of judgmental hostility,
and the ever-present possibility of world annihilation.
Peace is a difficult priority.
It means selflessness. It means suffering.

Help me, Prince of Peace, to become an active peacemaker.
Let me begin in my own home.
Yet do not let me limit my peace efforts
to a world so small that it includes no obligation
except to my chosen circle.

May your mother's concern
for your Mystical Body
be my courage
in the martyrdom
of peacemaking.

The Fourteenth Station
Jesus Is Entombed

They bury him.
He, for whom there had been no room in the inn (Luke 2:7),
had to be buried in someone else's tomb (Matt. 27:60).
Gethsemane of the bloody sweat.
Jerusalem of the bloodthirsty condemnation.
Golgotha of the bloodletting death.
But this place?
Not even a name.

The Justice of Jesus

Not even a name.
"In the place where he was crucified there was a garden,
and in the garden a new tomb" (John 19:41).
Not even a brief biography of birth and death to mark the stone.
Not the slightest thought of an Easter.

We stare at the tomb.
The injustice of it all!
The tomb tells its own story.
A tale of brutality,
of disregard,
of gluttonous self-interest,
of high-handed disdain.

The story that cries out for the work of justice.
Tirelessly. Relentlessly.

The tomb.
Thousands of years in stony sleep.
Now it yawns to receive its Creator.
A cruel awakening.

The tomb.
Dug out by the clawing fingers of greed.
Fingers that grasp at life with unutterable selfishness.
Injustice had killed him. Injustice buries him.
The end, apparently.

"It is finished" (John 19:30).
His cry from the cross.
And it was indeed.

But not like a book is finished and the cover is closed on the last chapter.
It was finished like bread is finished baking and is ready to be eaten.
Like wine is finished aging and is ready to be tasted.
Like a child is finished in the womb and is ready to be born.

He is the seed buried in good soil (Matt. 13:8).
The yeast kneaded into the dough (Luke 13:21).
The mustard seed planted in the garden (Luke 13:19).

Justice.
His eternal concern.
The hungry.
The homeless.
The naked.
The prisoner.
The oppressed.
The poor.
"When you give a reception,
invite beggars and the crippled, the lame and the blind" (Luke 14:13).

His work is finished.
Ours is not.
Gaining divine justice for us is finished.
The distribution of that justice is not.

The words of consecration are finished.
The communion is not.
We cannot be satisfied with a private faith.
"Go into the whole world..." (Mark 16:15).
Our faith must do justice until his kingdom is totally finished.
His kingdom of justice.

We are his Body. His branches.
And there is so much to be done.
A kingdom fully established.
"Good teacher, what must I do to share in everlasting life?" (Luke 18:18).
He looked at the young man with love.
"Sell all you have... then come and follow me" (Luke 18:22).
Keeping the commandments isn't enough.

There are ideals to pursue:
Hungering and thirsting for justice (Matt. 5:6).
And in our work for justice we are to be
the "salt of the earth... light of the world" (Matt. 5:13–14).
Justice.
Our enduring concern.
Concern for working conditions where morals are safeguarded.
Where physical well-being is not endangered.
Where young people's development is not impaired.

Concern for the right to participate in the political process.
To have an equal share of resources so as to live in dignity.
To enjoy freedom of movement and residence.
To have access to necessary information.
Concern for the eradication of hunger and disease,
ignorance and oppression, economic slavery and warmaking expediency.
Working for justice means efforts to preserve and enhance
the dignity of human beings.
And their basic human rights.

The gospel ideal of love is pursued
by applying the virtue of social justice
to our complex human relationships.

Justice. Too many of us stop with the tomb. Bury ourselves.
Don't want to be made aware of worldwide injustice.
Or be involved in local, social justice issues.
Too many are smug in their comfortable lifestyles.
Even worse. Their minds are closed. Their attitudes are frozen.
They deal in mutual exclusives.
Confronted with different ideas or different issues,
different problem-solving methods or different involvements,
they become entrenched in intolerance.
Their "either-or" mentality breeds hostile rash judgments.
Hateful condemnations. Belligerent self-righteousness.
Hardly the attitude that accomplishes justice.

If theirs is to be a faith that does justice,
they need to be brought to a "both-and" mentality.
Open to the possibility that the other person may be right.
Aware that there is more than one way.

A "both-and" mentality that makes room for variety.
Thrives on differences. Grows through creative exchanges.
That advocates pluralism:
A person who disagrees on a fundamental issue
need not have his or her entire value system vitiated.
Need not be totally condemned. He told us clearly:
The work of justice is essentially linked to faith. Ours to do.
"Seek first his Kingdom and his justice" (Matt. 6:33).

88

Prayer

Jesus, your death revealed the power of evil,
exposed the evil of the unjust.
By becoming sin for us, you became "the justice of God."
And so did we (2 Cor. 5:21).

How I need your strength to work for justice. I need your power.
Release me from my ease, my indifference.
Help me to expand my concern to include those faceless masses —
destitute because of callous profiteering,
wrecked because of our inhumanity toward one another.

Disturb me so that I will recognize the causal relationship
between my lifestyle and the injustices that entomb the deprived of the world.

Jesus, I am so weak. I don't want to know. Or get involved.

Make my life an endless effort at seeing into the meaning of your tomb;
my reflections a probing into your death that is life-giving;
my worship a celebration proclaiming your death until you come.
Jesus, I believe that there ultimately will be justice.
I believe that death, which forgets so tolerantly,
will always remember as long as there is bread and wine.

May your life-giving death
be my faith-doing justice.

The Fifteenth Station
Jesus Is Risen

S o many words ready to burst forth.
Words of poets.
Words of philosophers.
Words of scientists.
Words of musicians.
Words of theologians.
Words of artists.
All waiting to be born.
Words eager to give birth to the one immortal idea of all ages.
And the only words that find life are so simple, so brief,
so uncomplicated that many great minds have overlooked them:
"He has risen!" (Mark 16:6).
The Word is risen.

The Persuasion of Jesus

91

The Word is risen.
The Word made flesh, made sin, made passion, made death, is risen.
We contemplate "the place where they laid him" (Mark 16:6).

Jesus of Bethlehem. Now the eternal man.
Jesus of Nazareth. Now the everlasting Galilean.
Jesus of Jerusalem. Now the Lord of the universe.
Jesus of Palestine. Now the Savior of the world.
Jesus of Golgotha. Now the cosmic Christ.

He who emptied himself of his divine dignity (Phil. 2:7)
has now emptied the tomb of his human humiliation.
"He is not here" (Mark 16:6).
He has risen!
Creative words.
Words of life.
Immortal words.
Words of destiny.
Living words.
Words of "good news."
And the good news is that he is alive.
Now.
This very moment. In my life.
"I live, yet not I,
but Christ is living in me" (Gal. 2:20).

Alive. In me.
With all the power of his persuasive love.
Urging.
Luring.
Gathering.
Leading.
Strengthening.
Drawing.
Forgiving.
Feeding.
Healing.
Identifying.
"I have come that they may have life
and have it to the full" (John 10:10).

Alive. In me.
"For me to live is Christ" (Phil. 1:21).
With all the force of his creative hope.
Renewing.
Revealing.
Inspiring.
Evolving.
Exploring.
Imagining.
Resurrecting.
Upholding.
Enlightening.
Uplifting.
Ascending.
"If you have been raised with Christ,
seek the things that are above" (Col. 3:1).

He persuades us with his resurrection power
to cause resurrections in the lives of others.
Help others to come alive.
To God.
To the world.
To people.
To themselves.
To draw others to that fullness of life
for which he laid down his life.

To cause resurrections in others will at times demand silence.
At other times, prophecy.
Will challenge us to sacrifice.
To willingness.
To need.
To justice.
To compassion.
To missionary courage.
To peacemaking mysticism.
And always to a sharing love ever seeking perfection.

"Christ now raised from the dead will never die again" (Rom. 6:9).
Yet in his members he is still being persecuted.

Crucified.
He persuades. He is rejected.
So often. By so many.
His persuasive love is always being offered.
It is not always accepted.

"See, I make all things new" (Rev. 21:5).

How we pervert his power!
We continue to pour our creative efforts:

Into the development of newer and more destructive weapons,
no matter what the consequences will be
for all those priceless lives for which he died and rose.

Into the amassing of newer and bigger multinational fortunes,
no matter what the cost will be for those already existing in dire poverty.

Into newer and more advanced technology,
no matter how the world's resources will be exploited
or what dangers there will be to a health-sustaining environment.

Into newer and more subliminal techniques of advertising,
no matter what our selfish consumerism will do to those bereft of life's essentials.

His resurrection love whispers persuasively.
How often do we listen?

Prayer

Jesus, risen Lord of the universe, your resurrection power never forces.
You always persuade. "Will you also go away?" (John 6:67).
With Peter I respond, "To whom shall we go?" (John 6:68).

Help me to follow your gentle persuasion. To enter into your resurrection.
Into your life out of death. That I may experience holiness out of sin.
Hope out of despair. Joy out of depression. Faith out of doubt.
Happiness out of loneliness. Love out of indifference. Zeal out of apathy.
Concern out of selfishness. Prayer out of frenzy. Involvement out of fear.
Justice out of carelessness. Peace out of greed.

So often I feel frustrated. Overloaded with burning issues. Helpless.
Your resurrection power in my life enables me to exclaim with Paul,
"I can do all things in him who strengthens me" (Phil. 4:13).
I am in you. You are in me. Persuading me.
Offering me the power to use my creative ability to "make all things new."

In the face of the injustice and lack of peace in the world,
I can still maintain optimism.
Your victory in us will eventually and ultimately
overcome all our sinful social structures.
Provided that we cooperate with you by trying to cause resurrections.
In the despairing. The alienated. The marginal. The poor. The despised.
The crucified members of your cosmic Body.
Help me by your persuasive love to become all you want me to become.
That I may share myself fully with those in any kind of need.

May your resurrection
be my persuasive words
of peace and justice.

95